Crochet for Christmas

Maumelle AR • Leisure Arts Inc.

1
2
3
4
5
6
7
8
9
10
11
12
HOLLY

CROCHET FOR CHRISTMAS

The Christmas season becomes even more festive when you are surrounded by holiday decorations. The designs in this leaflet can be made and displayed in your home, given as gifts, or presented as bazaar items.

In addition to being seasonally attractive, some of the designs allow you to utilize items which often are discarded, such as coffee cans, juice cans and hosiery containers.

If you have any difficulty understanding the instructions or have a problem with any of the patterns, please write to us; we will make every effort to assist you. We would also enjoy hearing your comments on this leaflet and your suggestions for other patterns you'd like to have us publish.

Design Department

GENERAL INSTRUCTIONS

GAUGE

To test your gauge, make up a 4" square sample swatch in the pattern stitch specified. Then measure it, counting your stitches and rows carefully. If you have more stitches per inch than specified, try again with a size larger hook; if fewer, try again with a size smaller hook. Keep trying until you find the size that will give you the specified gauge. Hook sizes given in instructions are merely given as guides and should never be used without making a sample swatch to check gauge.

IMPORTANT

The gauge specified in the pattern instructions for **Mr. & Mrs. Snowman, Santa Bank, Santa Claus Ornament and Pine Cones** must be achieved so that the finished pieces will properly fit the container which they cover.

INCREASING AND DECREASING METHODS USED IN PATTERNS

Increasing—In a plain pattern of single or double crochet, an increase is made by working two stitches in one stitch.

Decreasing in Single Crochet—Work a single crochet until there are 2 loops on hook ***(Fig. 1)***; insert hook in next stitch, YO and draw through st: 3 loops now on hook ***(Fig. 2)***. YO and draw through all 3 loops at one time: dec made.

Fig. 1

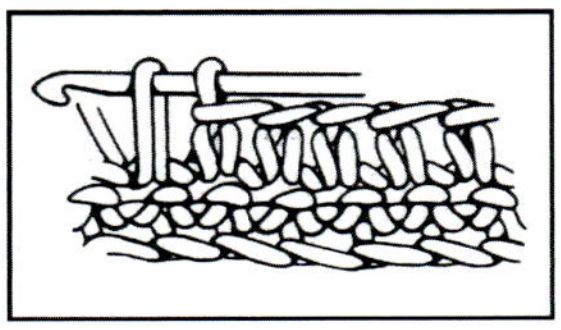

Fig. 2

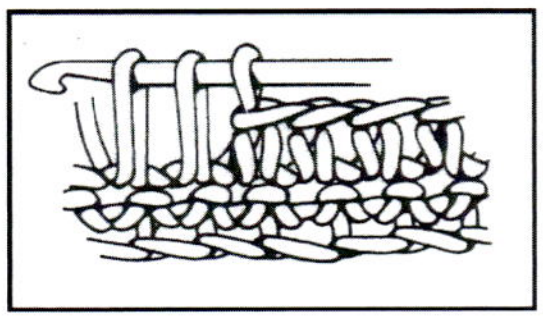

Decreasing in Double Crochet—Work a double crochet until there are 2 loops on hook. Keeping the 2 loops on hook, YO and insert hook in next st; YO and draw through st: 4 loops now on hook ***(Fig. 3)***. YO and draw through 2 loops: 3 loops rem on hook ***(Fig. 4)***. YO and draw through all 3 loops at one time: dec made.

Fig. 3

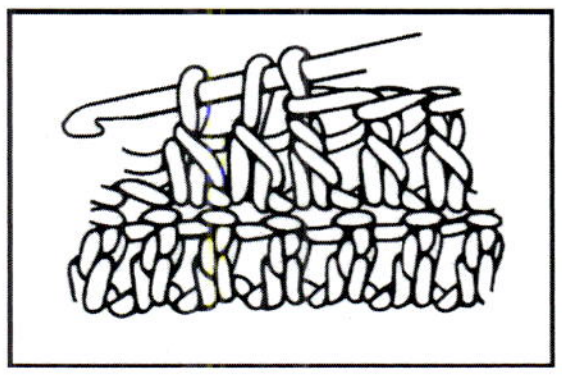

Fig. 4

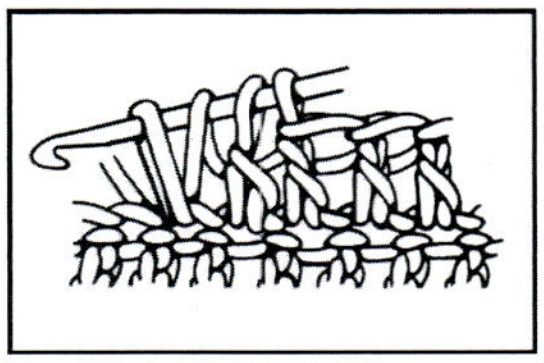

POMPONS

To make a pompon, cut two cardboard circles, each 2" in diameter, or size of desired finished pompon. Cut a center hole about ½" in diameter (larger for larger pompon; smaller for smaller pompon) in each circle. Thread yarn needle with doubled 72" length of yarn, and holding circles together, pass needle through center hole, over outside edge, through center again ***(Fig. 5)*** until entire circle is covered. You will need to use more lengths of yarn to complete pompon.

With very sharp scissors, cut yarn between the edge of the two circles ***(Fig. 6)***. Using a 12" strand of yarn doubled, slip yarn between cardboard circles, pull up tightly and tie very firmly. Remove cardboards and fluff out pompon by rolling between your hands. Trim with scissors to even off. Thread tying ends into yarn needle and attach pompon firmly.

Fig. 5

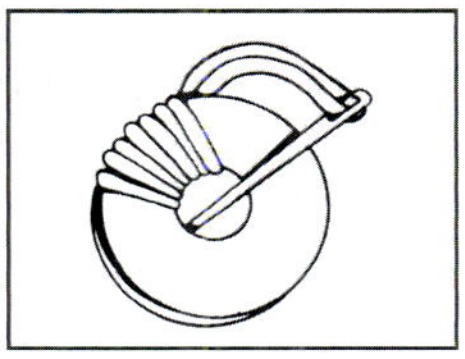

Fig. 6

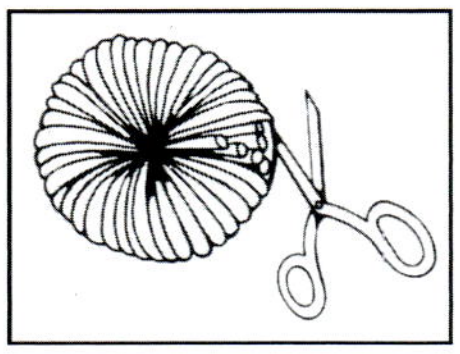

Photographed items made by Nancy Burnet, Judy Demain, Joan Kokaska, Wanda Parker, Kathie Schroeder, Janice Tessitore and Mary Thomas.

1 WREATH ORNAMENT

designed by Barbara Luoma; Mundelein, IL

Size: Approx 4" diameter

Materials: Worsted wt yarn, few yds **each** of green and red; aluminum crochet hook size E (Canadian size 9); 2½" curtain ring.

Gauge: None specified

PATTERN STITCH

Double Knot Stitch: ★ Draw up loop now on hook to measure ½", YO and draw through loop, insert hook between ½" loop and the single strand behind it ***(Fig. 7)***, YO and draw yarn through: 2 loops now on hook; YO, draw through both loops on hook tightly forming top knot of double knot st **(single knot st just made)**; rep from ★ once. You have now completed one double knot st.

Fig. 7

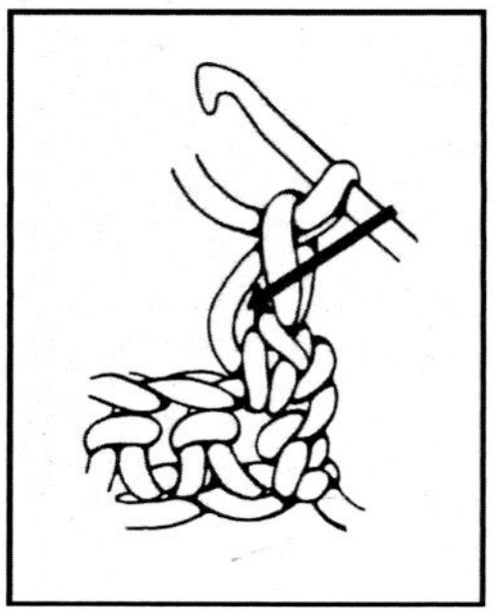

INSTRUCTIONS

With green, make a slip knot and sl st into curtain ring.

Rnd 1: Work 48 sc into ring, join with a sl st in first sc.

Rnd 2: Ch 1, sc in same st, make a double knot st following Patt St instructions above; ★★ sk 3 sc, sc in next sc, make a double knot st; rep from ★★ around, join by inserting hook in top knot of first double knot st at beg of rnd, work 1 tight sc.

Rnd 3: Make a double knot st in each st around by working into top knot of each double knot st of prev rnd ***(Fig. 8)***, ending with a sl st in first double knot st of rnd.

Finish off.

Finishing: With red, ch 100 for bow. Weave chain in and out of first row of double knot sts, tie in a bow.

Fig. 8

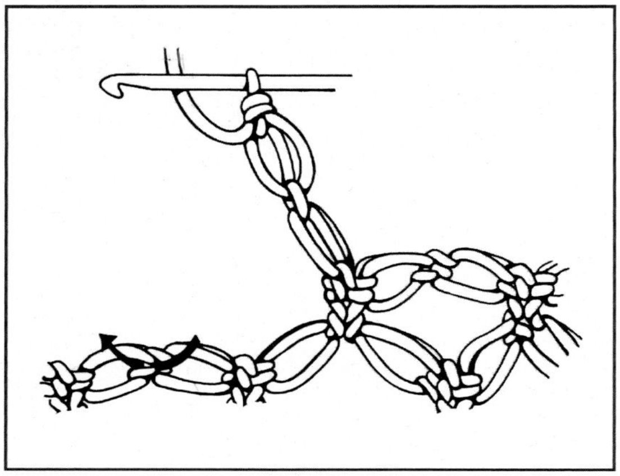

2 SANTA CLAUS ORNAMENT

designed by Barbara Luoma; Mundelein, IL

Materials: Worsted wt yarn, 1 oz **each** of red, wh te and pink, 1 yd of black; steel crochet hook sizes 1 and 2 (Canadian sizes 0 and 1); egg-shaped hosiery container; sewing thread for finishing.

Gauge: With smaller hook,
in sc, 10 sts = 2"; 12 rows = 2"
With larger hook, in sc, 4 sts =1"; 5 rows =1"

INSTRUCTIONS

Head: With pink and smaller hook, ch 2.

NOTE: Throughout patt, unless otherwise specified, ***do not*** *join rnds; mark beg of each rnd and move marker at end of each rnd. Marking will not be mentioned again.*

Rnd 1: 8 Sc in 2nd ch from hook.

Rnd 2: 2 Sc in each sc around: 16 sc.

Rnd 3: 2 sc in each sc around: 32 sc.

Rnds 4 and 5: Sc in each sc.

Rnd 6: ★ Sc in each of next 2 sc, 2 sc in next sc; rep from ★ around: 42 sc.

Rnds 7-28: Sc in each sc.

INSERT EGG-SHAPED CONTAINER.

Rnd 29: ★ Dec over next 2 sc; rep from ★ around: 21 sc.

Rnds 30 and 31: Rep Rnd 29, twice: 6 sc.

Finish off.

Hat: With red and larger hook, ch 40, join with a sl st to form a ring.

Rnd 1: Sc in same st and in each ch around: 40 sc.

Rnds 2-9: Sc in each sc.

Rnd 10: ★ Sc in each of next 6 sc, dec; rep from ★ around: 35 sc.

Rnd 11: ★ Sc in each of next 5 sc, dec; rep from ★ around: 30 sc.

Rnd 12: ★ Sc in each of next 4 sc, dec; rep from ★ around: 25 sc.

Rnds 13-18: Sc in each sc.

Rnd 19: ★ Sc in each of next 3 sc, dec; rep from ★ around: 20 sc.

Rnd 20: Sc in each sc.

Rnd 21: ★ Sc in each of next 2 sc, dec; rep from ★ around: 15 sc.

Rnds 22-26: Sc in each sc.

Rnd 27: ★ Sc in next sc, dec; rep from ★ around: 10 sc.

Rnds 28-31: Sc in each sc.

Rnd 32: Dec in each st around: 5 sc.

Rnd 33: Sc in each sc; finish off.

Hat Band: With white and larger hook, ch 42.

Row 1: Sc in 2nd ch from hook and in each ch across; ch 1, turn.

Row 2: Sc in each sc across; ch 1, turn.

Row 3: Rep Row 2, do **not** ch 1; finish off.

Moustache: With white and larger hook, ch 12, sl st in 2nd ch from hook and in each of next 9 ch across, work 2 sl st in last ch; hook beg yarn tail and draw through loop now on hook.

Finish off.

Eyes (make 2): With white and larger hook, ch 2, 5 sc in 2nd ch from hook; finish off.

Pompons (make 6): Following pompon instructions on page 3, make 6 fat 1¼" diameter pompons.

Finishing: Sew hat band to bottom of hat.

Sew one pompon to tip of hat, stitch hat to head.

Tack down side of hat. See close-up photo ***(Fig. 9)*** for placement of facial features.

Stitch eyes in place; with black yarn, work one french knot in center of each eye.

With pink yarn, work several straight sts horizontally for nose. Sew moustache below nose, turning up slightly at corners; at midpoint of moustache, sew and draw center sts tog tightly.

With red yarn, work a few straight sts below center of moustache for mouth. String 5 rem pompons tog and sew to bottom of head for beard.

Ch 30 for hanger; fold in half and attach cut ends to top of hat.

Fig. 9

3 SNOWFLAKES

designed by Margaret Dobson Druse; Easton, PA

Materials: #20 crochet cotton, 250-yd ball white; steel crochet hook size 8; tracing paper; pencil; rust-proof steel straight pins or T-pins; boiled or sugar-and-water starch; cardboard or ironing board for blocking.

Gauge: None specified; slightly smaller or larger size hooks make minimal difference.

SPOKED SNOWFLAKE (approx 4" diameter)

Ch 8, join with a sl st to form a ring.

Rnd 1: Ch 3, work 11 dc in ring, join with a sl st in top of beg ch.

Rnd 2: Ch 4, tr in same st as joining, 2 tr in next st, ch 1, ★ 2 tr in each of next 2 sts, ch 1; rep from ★ around, join with a sl st to top of beg ch.

Rnd 3: Ch 1, sc in same st. ★ Sc in next tr, sl st in next tr; ch 13, sc in 4th ch from hook, ch 4, sc in same st, ch 3, sl st in 3rd ch from hook, sl st in same st with two prev scs; sc in each of next 3 ch sts. **First arm of spoke completed.** ★★ Ch 7, sc in 4th ch from hook, ch 4, sc in same st, ch 3, sl st in 3rd ch from hook, sl st in same st with prev scs, sc in each of next 3 ch sts. **Center arm of spoke completed.** Rep from ★★ once, join with a sl st in same st with base of first arm; sc in each of next 6 ch sts. Sc in top of tr at beg of ch-13 (this will be the third tr in the group of four). Sc in top of next tr, sc in ch-1 sp, ch 4, sl st in 4th ch from hook for picot, sc in next tr; rep from ★ around, join with a sl st in first sc of rnd.

Finish off.

Alternate Rnd 3: For each spoke, ch 16 instead of 13 and sl st instead of sc to make thinner spokes.

PICOT CLUSTER SNOWFLAKE (approx 4¾" diameter)

Ch 5, join with a sl st to form a ring.

Rnd 1: Ch 4 (counts as first dc and ch 1), ★ dc in ring, ch 1; rep from ★ 10 times, join with a sl st in 3rd ch of beg ch.

Rnd 2: ★ Ch 3, sl st in top of next dc; rep from ★ around, join with a sl st in base of beg ch: 12 loops made.

Rnd 3: Ch 4, tr in same st, ★ ch 7, sk 2 loops, 2 tr in next sl st; rep from ★ around, ch 7, sk 2 loops, join with a sl st in top of beg ch.

Rnd 4: Ch 1, sc in same st, ★ (ch 9, sc in 4th ch from hook) twice; ch 5, sl st in 4th ch from hook; (ch 4, sl st in same st) twice: **picot cluster made**. Ch 5, sl st in 4th ch from hook, sc in base of opposite picot; ch 9, sc in 4th ch from hook; ch 5, sc in top of next tr. Ch 9, sl st in 4th ch from hook, ch 5, sc in top of next tr. Rep from ★ around, join with a sl st in beg sc.

Finish off.

TREBLE CLUSTER SNOWFLAKE (approx 5" diameter)

Ch 5, join with a sl st to form a ring.

Rnd 1: Ch 4 (counts as first tr), work 2 tr in ring, ch 2, ★ 3 tr in ring, ch 2; rep from ★ 4 times, join with a sl st in top of beg ch: 6 clusters made with ch 2 between each.

Rnd 2: Ch 4, tr in each of next 2 tr, ch 6, ★ tr in each of next 3 tr, ch 6; rep from ★ 4 times, join with a sl st in top of beg ch-4: 6 clusters with ch 6 between.

Rnd 3: ★ Sl st in next tr; ch 14, sc in 12th ch from hook; ch 12, sc in 10th ch from hook; ch 10, sc in 8th ch from hook; ch 8, sl st in 6th ch from hook, ch 6, sl st in same st at base of ch. Now working the opposite side of ch, ch 5, sl st in same st at base of ch, sl st in each of next 2 ch sts and in sc of opposite loop; ch 7, sl st again in same sc, sl st in each of next 2 chs and in sc of opposite loop; ch 9, sl st again in same sc, sl st in each of next 2 chs and in sc of opposite loop; ch 11, sl st again in same sc, sl st in each of next 2 chs. Sl st in top of tr with beg ch-14 **(center tr of cluster)**. Sl st in next tr, 3 sc in next ch-6 loop; ch 3, sl st in 3rd ch from hook, (ch 3, sl st in same st at base of ch) twice: **picot cluster made**. 3 sc in same ch-6 loop, sl st in next tr; rep from ★ around, join with a sl st.

Finish off.

Finishing: Prepare starch, using a commercial starch or a sugar-and-water starch made as follows.

Mix ½ cup granulated sugar with ½ cup water in a small pan. Heat to boiling (be careful not to burn) and immediately remove from heat. Cool to room temperature.

Fig. 10

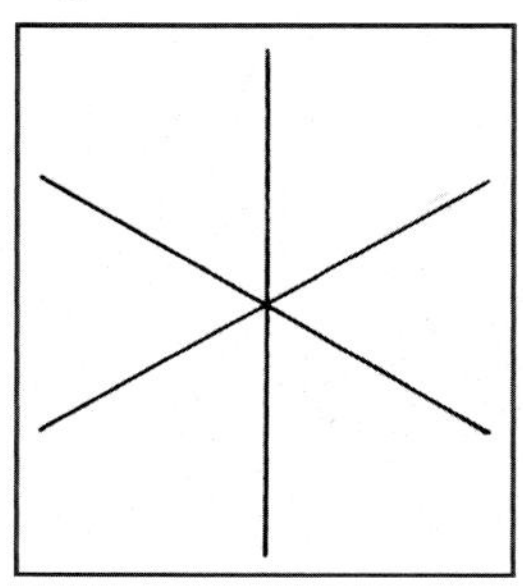

Fig. 11

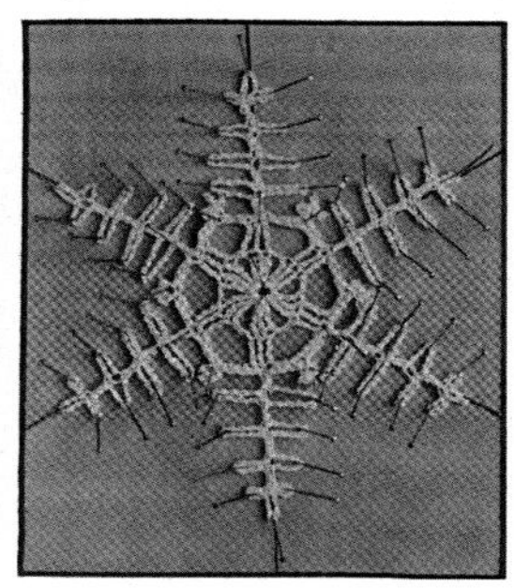

Make outlines for blocking as follows. Place tracing paper over ***Fig. 10***. With pencil, trace over the lines, using a ruler and extending the lines out to the desired length. Use a separate sheet of paper for each snowflake to be blocked.

Wet each snowflake in clear water, then immerse in starch. Remove snowflakes from starch and place on paper; insert one pin in center of snowflake and center of outline. Now insert pins at outermost points, and points between, stretching as far as they will go ***(Fig. 11)***.

Allow snowflakes to dry thoroughly before removing pins. Make loop hangers from white or translucent nylon thread.

4 PLACEMAT & NAPKIN RING

designed by Barbara Luoma; Mundelein, IL

Size: Placemat, approx 16" x 12"
Napkin Ring, approx 1½" diameter, 2¼" wide

Materials: Worsted wt yarn, 2 oz white, 1 oz **each** red and green, small amount of gold for center of flower; aluminum crochet hook sizes E and G (Canadian sizes 9 and 7) or size needed for gauge; sewing thread for finishing.

Gauge: With larger hook, in patt of (2 dc, ch 1), 4 patts and 5 rows= 2¾"

INSTRUCTIONS

PLACEMAT

With white and larger hook, ch 64.

Row 1: Dc in 4th ch from hook, ★ ch 1, sk next ch, dc in each of next 2 chs; rep from ★ across, ch 4, turn.

Row 2: ★ 2 Dc in next ch-1 sp, ch 1; rep from ★ across, ending dc in top of turning ch, ch 3, turn.

Row 3: Dc in first sp, ★ ch 1, 2 dc in next sp; rep from ★ across, ending 2 dc in last sp, ch 4, turn.

Rep Rows 2 and 3 for a total of 20 rows.

Finish off.

Edging: Before working edging rnds, work one row of sl st loosely across each short end of placemat as follows:

★ With right side facing and short end across top, join white with a sl st in upper, right-hand corner; work 2 sl sts in each row across: 40 sts. Finish off. Rep from ★ for other short end.

Rnd 1: With right side facing and long end across top, join red with a sl st at upper, right-hand corner in first ch-1 sp, ★ ch 3, sc in next ch-1 sp; rep from ★ to corner: 20 ch-3 loops. At corner, work (sc, ch 3, sc) in corner st. Across short end, work (ch 3, sk 2 sl sts, sc in next sl st) 13 times; at corner, work (sc, ch 3, sc) in corner st. Rep from ★ for next long end and short end, ending last rep by joining in beg st of rnd with a sl st. Finish off red.

Rnd 2: Join green with a sl st in any ch-3 sp, ★ ch 3, sc in next ch-3 sp; rep from ★ around, working (sc, ch 3, sc) in each corner ch-3 sp, join with a sl st in beg st of rnd.

Finish off.

Floral Motif Appliqué

Center: With gold and smaller hook, ch 2, work 8 sc in 2nd ch from hook, join with a sl st in first sc. Finish off.

Petals (make 8): ★ Join red with a sl st in any gold sc, ch 8, sc in 2nd ch from hook, hdc in next ch, dc in each of next 3 chs, hdc in next ch, sc in next ch. Turn work so that you can work in unworked loops on opposite side of beg ch: Sc in first ch, hdc in next ch, dc in each of next 3 chs, hdc in next ch, sc in next ch, join with a sl st in beg sc on opposite side; finish off: **one petal made.** Rep from ★ 7 times: 8 petals made.

Leaves (make 2): With green, ch 10.

Row 1: Sc in 2nd ch from hook, sc in each of next 7 chs, 3 sc in last ch. Now working in loops on opposite side of beg ch: Sc in each of next 6 sts, ch 1, turn.

***NOTE:** On following rows, work into back loop only* (BLO) *of each st.*

Row 2: Sk first sc, sc in each of next 6 sc, 3 sc in next sc, sc in each of next 6 sc on other side, ch 1, turn.

Row 3: Sk first sc, sc in each of next 6 sc, 3 sc in next sc, sc in each of next 6 sc on other side, ch 1, turn.

Row 4: Sk first sc, sc in each of next 6 sc, 3 sc in next sc, sc in each of next 6 sc on other side. Finish off.

Finishing: Hand sew flower to leaves; sew entire motif at corner of placemat.

Napkin Ring instructions begin on page 8.

NAPKIN RING

With larger hook and white, ch 18, join with a sl st to form a ring.

Rnd 1: Ch 3, dc in next ch, ★ ch 1, sk next ch, dc in each of next 2 chs; rep from ★ around, ending ch 1, join with a sl st in top of beg ch.

Rnd 2: Sl st to next ch-1 sp, ch 3, dc in same sp, ★ ch 1, 2 dc in next ch-1 sp; rep from ★ around, ending ch 1, join with a sl st in top of beg ch. Finish off.

Edging - Rnd 1: Join red in any ch-1 sp with a sl st, ★ ch 3, sc in next ch-1 sp; rep from ★ around, join with a sl st in beg sl st. Finish off red.

Rnd 2: Join green with a sl st in any ch-3 loop, ★ ch 3, sc in next ch-3 loop; rep from ★ around, join with a sl st in beg sl st. Finish off green.

Rep Edging Rnds 1 and 2 for other end of napkin ring.

Floral Motif Appliqué

Center: With gold and smaller hook, ch 2, 6 sc in second ch from hook, join with a sl st in beg sc. Finish off.

Petals (make 6): ★ Join red with a sl st in any gold sc, ch 6, sc in second ch from hook, hdc in next ch, dc in next ch, hdc in next ch, sc in next ch; turn. Now working in loops on opposite side of beg ch; sc in next ch, hdc in next ch, dc in next ch, hdc in next ch, sc in next st on other side, sl st in beg sc; finish off: **one petal made**. Rep from ★ 5 times: 6 petals made.

Leaves (make 2): With green, ch 7.

Row 1: Sc in 2nd ch from hook and in each of next 4 chs, 3 sc in last ch. Now working in loops on opposite side of beg ch: Sc in each of next 3 ch, ch 1, turn.

Row 2: Sk first sc, sc in BLO of each of next 3 sc, 3 sc in BLO of next sc, sc in BLO of each of next 4 sc, ch 1, turn.

Row 3: Sk first sc, sc in BLO of next 4 sc, 3 sc in BLO of next sc, sc in BLO of next 3 sc. Finish off.

Finishing: Hand sew flower to leaves; sew entire motif on napkin ring.

5 SANTA BANK

designed by Barbara Luoma; Mundelein, IL

Materials: Worsted wt yarn, 4 oz red, 4 oz white, 1 oz **each** pink and black; aluminum crochet hook sizes E and F (Canadian sizes 9 and 8) or sizes needed for gauge; 2-lb coffee can with plastic lid; polyester filling for stuffing head and arms; sewing thread for finishing.

Gauge: With smaller hook, in sc, 9 sts = 2"; 10 rows = 2"
With larger hook, in sc, 4 sts = 1"; 5 rows = 1"

*NOTE: Throughout patt, unless otherwise specified, **do not** join at ends of rnds; mark beg of each rnd and move marker at end of each rnd. Joining will not be mentioned again until instructions for Hat.*

INSTRUCTIONS

Body: Beg at top with red and smaller hook, ch 2.

Rnd 1: Work 8 sc in 2nd ch from hook. Mark last st for end of rnd.

Rnd 2: 2 Sc in each sc around: 16 sc.

Rnd 3: Sc in each sc.

Rnd 4: 2 Sc in each sc: 32 sc.

Rnd 5: Sc in each sc.

Rnd 6: ★ 2 sc in next sc, sc in next sc; rep from ★ around: 48 sc.

Rnd 7: Sc in each of next 2 sc, sl st loosely across next 10 sc, sc in each rem sc around.

Rnd 8: Hdc in first sc, dc in next sc, ch 12, sk 10 sl sts, dc in next sc, hdc in next sc **(you have just formed the coin slot)**; sc in each rem sc around: 50 sc.

Work even in sc until piece measures 5" from end of Rnd 8.

Finish off, leaving 36" length of yarn for sewing to bottom later.

Bottom: With red and smaller hook, work Rnds 1-6 as for Body.

Rnds 7 and 8: Sc in each sc.

Rnd 9: 2 Sc in first sc, sc in each of next 23 sc; 2 sc in next sc; sc in each sc around: 50 sc.

Work even in sc until piece measures 3" from end of Rnd 9.

Finish off.

Bands for Jacket and Hat: All bands are worked with white yarn and **larger** hook.

Waistband: Ch 72.

Row 1: Sc in 2nd ch from hook and in each ch across; ch 1, turn: 71 sc.

Rows 2-5: Sc in each sc across; ch 1, turn. At end of last row, do not ch; finish off.

Center Front Band: Ch 14.

Row 1: Sc in 2nd ch from hook and in each ch across; ch 1, turn: 13 sc.

Rows 2-5: Sc in each sc; ch 1, turn. At end of last row, do not ch; finish off.

Sleeve Bands (make 2): Ch 18.

Row 1: Sc in 2nd ch from hook and in each ch across; ch 1, turn: 17 sc.

Row 2: Sc in each sc; ch 1, turn.

Row 3: Sc in each sc; finish off.

Hat Band: Ch 51.

Row 1: Sc in 2nd ch from hook and in each ch across; ch 1, turn: 50 sc.

Rows 2-4: Sc in each sc; ch 1, turn. At end of last row, do not ch; finish off.

Head: Start at top with pink and smaller hook.

Rnd 1: Ch 2, 8 sc in 2nd ch from hook. Mark last st for end of rnd.

Rnds 2 and 3: 2 Sc in each sc around: 32 sc at end of Rnd 3.

Rnds 4-6: Sc in each sc.

Rnd 7: Sc in each of next 2 sc, ★ 2 sc in next sc, sc in each of next 2 sc; rep from ★ around: 42 sc.

Rnds 8-20: Sc in each sc.

Rnd 21: ★ Sc in each of next 4 sc, dec; rep from ★ around: 35 sc.

Rnds 22-26: Rep Rnd 21. At end of Rnd 26, you should have 15 sc.

Finish off, leaving 8" length of yarn for sewing.

Arms (make 2): Beg at mittens with black and smaller hook, ch 2.

Rnd 1: Work 8 sc in 2nd ch from hook. Mark last st for end of rnd.

Rnd 2: ★ 2 Sc in next sc, sc in next sc; rep from ★ around: 12 sc.

Rnds 3-8: Sc in each sc; on last st of Rnd 8, work off last loop with red; finish off black, continue with red.

For ease in finishing later, you may wish to stuff arms as you work the following rnds.

Rnds 9-39: Sc in each sc. Finish off, leaving 10" length of yarn for sewing.

Hat: Beg at bottom of hat with red and **larger** hook, ch 43. Join with a sl st to form a ring.

NOTE: Join and mark end of each rnd for this piece.

Rnd 1: Sc in 2nd ch from hook and in each ch around: 42 sc.

Rnds 2-9: Sc in each sc.

Rnds 10-12: Sc in each sc, dec 5 sc evenly spaced, each rnd: 27 sc.

Rnds 13-22: Sc in each sc.

Rnd 23: Sc in each sc, dec 5 sc evenly spaced around: 22 sc.

Rnds 24 and 25: Sc in each sc.

Rnd 26: Sc in each sc, dec 5 sc evenly spaced around: 17 sc.

Rnds 27-29: Sc in each sc.

Rnd 30: Sc in each sc, dec 5 sc evenly spaced around: 12 sc.

Rnds 31-36: Sc in each sc.

Rnd 37: Sc in each sc, dec 3 sc evenly spaced around: 9 sc.

Rnds 38 and 39: Sc in each sc.

Rnd 40: Sc in each sc, dec 4 sc evenly spaced around: 5 sc.

Finish off.

Eyes (make 2): With white and larger hook, ch 2, 5 sc in 2nd ch from hook; finish off.

Moustache: With white and larger hook, ch 12, sl st in 2nd ch from hook and in each of next 10 ch across, work 2 sl sts in last ch; hook beg yarn tail and draw through loop now on hook. Finish off.

Pompons: Following instructions on page 3, make 11 fat 1½" diameter pompons.

Finishing: With sharp-pointed scissors, cut slit in can lid to correspond to slot opening in top of body. Tape lid down on can. Pull body down over top of can so that slot opening is over slit in can lid. Insert can into bottom, stretching piece to fit. With yarn tail, seam the two pieces tog, carefully matching sts. Tack center front band in position vertically.
Tack waistband around the joining seam.

Arms: Stuff with polyester filling to within 1" from opening; sew arms tog at openings. Tack one sleeve band to end of each black mitten. Attach arm unit by tacking it directly in front of slot opening (about center of top of lid). With black, tack tips of mittens tog.

Head: Refer to close-up photo *(Fig. 12)* as a guide for placement of facial features.

Sew eyes in place and work one french knot with black yarn for center of each eye.

With pink, work several horizontal straight sts for nose.

Sew moustache horizontally below nose, turning up slightly at corners; at midpoint, sew and draw center sts tog just below nose.

With red, sew a few horizontal straight sts below center of moustache for mouth.

Stuff head firmly, sew opening closed.

Join hat band to bottom of hat; attach one pompon to tip of hat.

Sew hat to top of head.

Sew entire head unit to body.

Tack long end of hat down at side.

For beard, sew rem pompons in two rows of 5 pompons each, as shown in photo.

Fig. 12

6 SANTA CLAUS DOORKNOB COVER

designed by Janet Kozenchick; Janet's Knit Nook; Gary, IN

Materials: Mohair wt yarn, 1 oz white; worsted wt yarn, several yds **each** red and black; aluminum crochet hook size E (Canadian size 9); polyester filling for stuffing hat; 1/8" wide elastic, long enough to fit over doorknob with ends sewn tog to form a ring; sewing thread for finishing.

Gauge: None specified

PATTERN STITCH

Double Loop Stitch: With wrong side of work facing, and using two strands of yarn, insert hook into stitch and wind yarn twice around left index finger. Holding yarn at least 2" from work, insert hook into loop and free yarn on finger *(Fig. 13)* and pull through st on hook: 6 loops now on hook. Drop loops off finger, YO and pull through all 6 loops on hook: One double loop st made. (Loops will be on right side of work, facing away from you.)

Fig. 13

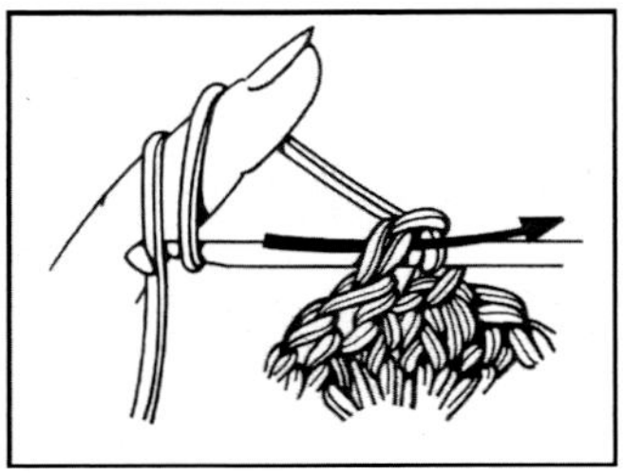

INSTRUCTIONS

Beg at center with white (using 2 strands here and throughout patt when using mohair wt yarn), ch 4; join with a sl st in first ch to form a ring.

Rnd 1: Ch 3, work 10 dc in ring, join with a sl st in top of beg ch-3; ch 1, turn.

Rnd 2: Work 2 double loop sts in each of next 7 sts, 2 sc in each of last 4 sts, sl st in beg st of rnd: 22 sts; ch 3, turn.

Rnd 3: Dc in base of ch, dc in next st, 2 dc in next st, ★ dc in each of next 3 dc, 2 dc in next st; rep from ★ around, ending dc in each of last 3 sts, join with a sl st in top of turning ch: 28 sts; ch 1, turn.

Rnd 4: Work 2 double loop sts in each of next 16 sts, sc in each of next 12 sts, join with a sl st in top of turning ch: 44 sts; ch 1, turn.

Rnd 5: Sc in each st around, join with a sl st in top of turning ch; ch 1, turn.

Rnd 6: ★ Sc in each of next 2 sts, dec; rep from ★ around, join with a sl st in top of turning ch: 33 sts; ch 1, turn.

Rnd 7: ★ Dec, sc in next st; rep from ★ around, join with a sl st in top of turning ch: 22 sts; ch 1, turn.

Rnd 8: Working over elastic ring, sc in each st around, join with a sl st in top of turning ch. Finish off.

Hat: With red, ch 4, join with a sl st to form a ring.

Rnd 1: Ch 3, work 10 dc in ring, join with a sl st in top of beg ch-3; ch 3, turn.

Rnd 2: Dc in base of ch, 2 dc in each st around, join with a sl st in top of turning ch: 22 dc; ch 3, turn.

Rnd 3: Dc in each dc around, join with a sl st in top of turning ch. Finish off, leaving 24" length for sewing.

Eyes (make 2): With black, ch 2; work 5 sc in 2nd ch from hook, join with a sl st in beg sc. Finish off.

Nose: With red, ch 2; work 4 sc in 2nd ch from hook, join with a sl st in beg sc. Finish off.

Finishing: Stuff hat lightly with polyester filling and sew to head. Make small pompon with double strand of white by winding yarn around finger 50 times, then slip off finger and tie in middle of bundle. Cut ends and trim. Sew to top of hat.

See close-up photo ***(Fig. 14)*** for placement of facial features.

Stitch eyes and nose in place.

Fig. 14

7 PINE CONES & BOW

designed by Barbara Luoma; Mundelein, IL

Materials: Worsted wt yarn, 4 oz brown, 1 oz green; aluminum crochet hook size D (Canadian size 10) or size needed for gauge; 3 egg-shaped hose containers.

Gauge: In dc, 4 sts = 1"; 2 rows = 1"

INSTRUCTIONS

Pine Cones (make 3): With brown, ch 2.

Rnd 1: 8 Sc in 2nd ch from hook; do not join.

Rnd 2: 2 Sc in each sc around; join with a sl st in beg sc of rnd: 16 sc.

Rnd 3: Sc ***loosely*** in each sc around; join with a sl st in beg sc of rnd.

Rnd 4: ★ Sc in next sc, shell of 3 dc in next sc, ch 1; rep from ★ around, join with a sl st in beg sc: 8 shells made.

Rnd 5: Holding first shell toward you and working behind it on wrong side, sl st loosely in back threads only at base of next dc ***(Fig. 15)***. Continuing to work on wrong side and at base of shell, insert hook from **back** to **front** through **bars** of center dc of shell and sl st into sc of rnd below (same st in which shell was worked), ***see Fig. 16***.

Fig. 15

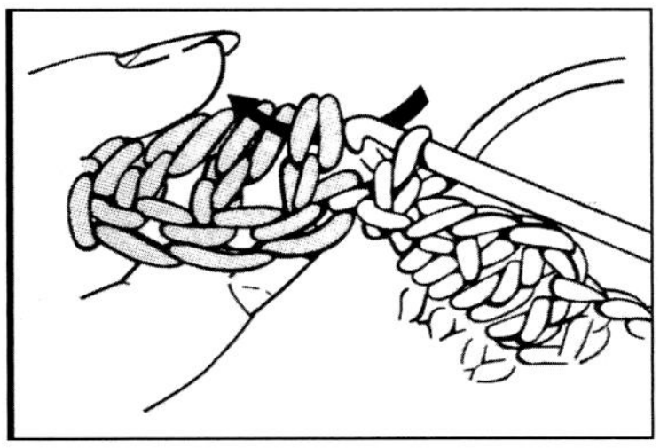

Fig. 16

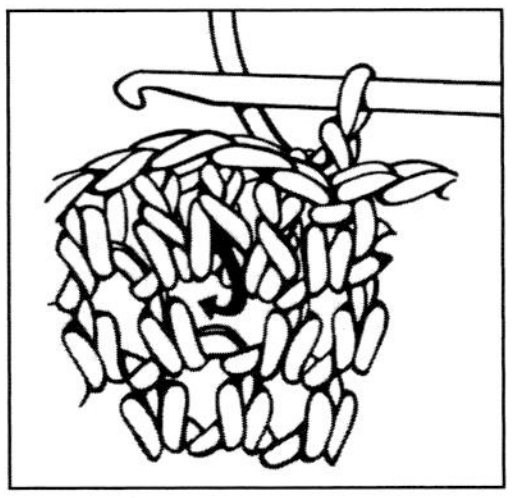

★ Ch 3, insert hook as before in center dc of next shell and sl st into sc in rnd below; rep from ★ around, ending ch 3, join with a sl st in sl st at base of first shell: 8 ch-3 loops made.

Rnd 6: ★ Ch 1, work shell of (sc, 5 dc, sc) in next ch-3 loop; rep from ★ around, ending ch 1, join with sl st in beg ch-1: 8 shells made.

Rnd 7: Working behind next shell as before, sl st in back threads only at base of each of first 3 sts, work an extended single crochet **(hereafter abbreviated ESC)** at center of shell, as follows: Insert hook from **back** to **front** through **bars** of center dc of shell *(Fig. 17);* then insert hook in back loop of ch-1 between shells in row below and pull loop through bars of dc to back of work; YO and draw yarn through pulled loop, YO and draw through rem 2 loops on hook: ESC made. ★ Ch 4, work 1 ESC in next shell as before; rep from ★ around, ending ch 4, join with a sl st in beg ESC of rnd.

Fig. 17

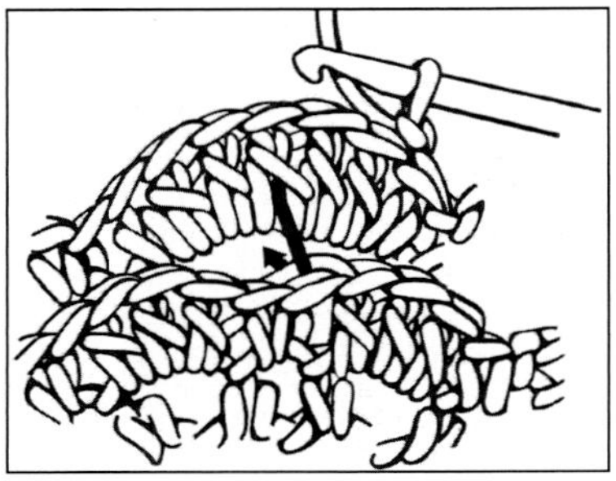

Rnd 8: Rep Rnd 6.

Rnd 9: Sl st in back of first 3 sts as before, work 1 ESC, ★ ch 5, ESC in next shell; rep from ★ around, ending ch 5, join in beg ESC.

Rnd 10: Rep Rnd 6.

Rnd 11: Sl st in back of first 3 sts as before, work 1 ESC, ★ ch 6, ESC in next shell; rep from ★ around, ending ch 6, join in beg ESC.

Rnds 12-21: Rep Rnds 8 and 9, 5 times.

Rnds 22-26: Rep Rnds 6 and 7 twice, then repeat Rnd 6 once **more.**

INSERT EGG-SHAPED CONTAINER.

Rnd 27: Sl st in back of first 3 sts, work 1 ESC, ★ ch 3, ESC in next shell; rep from ★ around, ending ch 3, join in beg ESC.

Rnd 28: Ch 1, ★ sc in center dc of next shell; rep from ★ around, join with a sl st in beg ch-1. Break yarn, leaving a 12" length; thread yarn needle, weave through sts and draw up tightly. Finish off.

Chains: With brown, make 3 chains.

First Chain: Ch 35, ★ sl st in 2nd ch from hook and in each ch across; finish off ★.

Second Chain: Ch 25, rep from ★ to ★.

Third Chain: Ch 10, rep from ★ to ★.

Bow: With green, ch 8.

Row 1: Dc in 4th ch from hook, dc in each of next 4 ch; ch 3, turn: 6 dc.

Rows 2-87: Dc in each st across; ch 3, turn. At end of last row, do not ch; finish off.

Finishing: Tie bow in center, attach pine cones to chains and chains to bow.

8 BELL ORNAMENTS

designed by Barbara Luoma; Mundelein, IL

Size: Approx 2½" high

Materials: Worsted wt yarn, 20 yds white, several yds each green and red; aluminum crochet hook size E (Canadian size 9); polyester filling for stuffing.

Gauge: None specified

INSTRUCTIONS

Bells (make 2): Beg at top with white, ch 2.

Rnd 1: 8 Sc in 2nd ch from hook, join with a sl st in beg sc.

Rnd 2: 2 Sc in same st as joining, 2 sc in each rem sc around, join with a sl st in beg sc: 16 sc.

Rnd 3: Ch 3 (counts as a dc), dc in each sc around, join with a sl st in top of beg ch-3.

Rnds 4-6: Ch 3, dc in each dc around, join with a sl st in top of beg ch-3: 16 dc.

Rnd 7: Ch 1, 5 hdc in next dc **(shell made),** ★ sc in next dc, shell in next dc; rep from ★ around, join with a sl st in beg ch-1. Finish off white.

Rnd 8: Join red with a sl st in same sp, sl st through both loops of each st around. Finish off red.

For second bell, rep Rnds 1-7; join green and rep Rnd 8. Finish off.

Clappers (make two): With white, ch 11.

Rnd 1: Sc in 2nd ch from hook and in each rem ch across; ch 1, turn.

Rnds 2-10: Sc in each sc; ch 1, turn. At end of Rnd 10, do not ch; finish off, leaving 8" length of yarn for closing.

Thread yarn needle, weave into every other st around all four sides, stuff and draw closed tightly. Finish off.

Finishing: Stuff top of bell.

Ties: Cut 2, 9" lengths of red yarn and 2, 9" lengths of green yarn. Attach one red and one green length of yarn to top of clapper, draw yarn through top of bell and knot. Rep for second bell, then knot the bells tog with ties by making one knot at top of bells and another knot at cut ends of yarn.

Bow: Using one 30" length each of red, green and white, make a braid and knot 2½" from each end. Use braided yarn to form a bow, attach to first knot at top of bells.

9 MR. & MRS. SNOWMAN

designed by Barbara Luoma; Mundelein, IL

Materials: Worsted wt yarn, 8 oz white, 2 oz black, 1 oz **each** green and brown, several yds red; aluminum crochet hook size E (Canadian size 9) or size needed for gauge; 1-lb coffee can; 46-oz juice can; seven 6" pipecleaners; polyester filling for stuffing: sewing thread for finishing.

Gauge: In sc, 10 sts = 2"; 11 rows = 2"

NOTE: Throughout patt, unless otherwise specified, ***do not*** *join rnds; mark beg of each rnd and move marker at end of each rnd. Marking will not be mentioned again in instructions.*

MR. SNOWMAN

BODY

Beg at bottom with white, ch 2.

Rnd 1: 8 Sc in 2nd ch from hook.

Rnd 2: 2 Sc in each sc around: 16 sc.

Rnd 3: Sc in each sc around.

Rnd 4: ★ 2 sc in next sc, sc in next sc; rep from ★ around: 24 sc.

Rnd 5: Sc in each sc around.

Rnd 6: ★ 2 Sc in next sc, sc in each of next 2 sc; rep from ★ around: 32 sc.

Rnd 7: ★ 2 Sc in next sc, sc in each of next 3 sc; rep from ★ around: 40 sc.

Rnd 8: ★ 2 Sc in next sc, sc in each of next 4 sc; rep from ★ around: 48 sc.

Rnd 9: ★ 2 Sc in next sc, sc in each of next 5 sc; rep from ★ around: 56 sc.

Rnd 10: ★ 2 sc in next sc, sc in each of next 6 sc; rep from ★ around: 64 sc.

Rnd 11: ★ 2 Sc in next sc, sc in each of next 7 sc; rep from ★ around: 72 sc. Join with a sl st in beg st of rnd; ch 1, turn.

Rnd 12: Work a raised sc as follows.

INSTRUCTIONS FOR RAISED SC: Insert hook in next st, now insert hook from *back* to *front* around the bars of same sc *(Fig. 18)*; hook yarn and pull through, YO and pull through 2 loops now on hook: one raised sc made.

Fig. 18

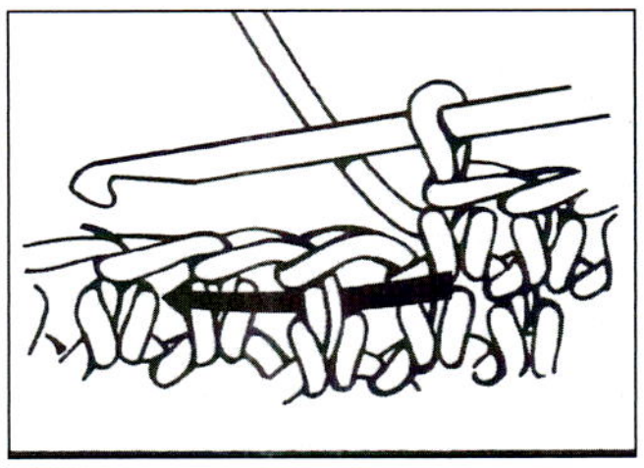

Work a raised sc in each rem st around, join with a sl st in beg st of rnd; turn.

Rnds 13-51: Sc in each sc around: 72 sc.

Rnd 52: ★ Sc in each of next 10 sc, dec; rep from ★ 5 times **more**: 66 sc.

Rnd 53: Sc in each sc around.

INSERT JUICE CAN.

Rnd 54: ★ Sc in each of next 9 sc, dec; rep from ★ 5 times **more**: 60 sc.

Rnds 55-57: Sc in each sc around.

Rnd 58: ★ Sc in each of next 8 sc, dec; rep from ★ 5 times **more**: 54 sc.

Rnd 59: Sc in each sc around.

Rnd 60: ★ Sc in each of next 7 sc, dec; rep from ★ 5 times **more**: 48 sc.

Rnd 61: Sc in each sc around.

Rnd 62: ★ Sc in each of next 6 sc, dec; rep from ★ 5 times **more**: 42 sc.

Rnd 63: Sc in each sc around.

Rnd 64: ★ Sc in each of next 5 sc, dec; rep from ★ 5 times **more**: 36 sc.

Rnd 65: Sc in each of next 36 sc, sl st in each of next 2 sc; finish off.

Stuff opening with polyester filling.

HEAD

Beg at top with white, ch 2.

Rnd 1: 8 Sc in 2nd ch from hook.

Rnd 2: 2 Sc in each sc around: 16 sc.

Rnd 3: 2 Sc in each sc around: 32 sc.

Rnds 4-6: Sc in each sc around.

Rnd 7: ★ 2 Sc in next sc, sc in next sc; rep from ★ around: 48 sc.

Rnds 8-16: Sc in each sc around.

Rnd 17: ★ Sc in each of next 10 sc, dec; rep from ★ around: 44 sc.

Rnd 18: Sc in each sc around.

Rnd 19: ★ Sc in each of next 9 sc, dec; rep from ★ around: 40 sc.

Rnd 20: Sc in each sc around.

Rnd 21: ★ Sc in each of next 8 sc, dec; rep from ★ around: 36 sc.

Rnds 22-23: Sc in each sc around, sl st in each of next 2 sc.

Finish off.

Eyes (make 2): With black, ch 2.

Rnd 1: 6 Sc in 2nd ch from hook.

Rnd 2: Sl st in each sc around, join with a sl st in first st of rnd; finish off.

Mouth: With red, ch 10; finish off.

Buttons (make 3): With black, ch 2.

Rnd 1: 8 Sc in 2nd ch from hook.

Rnd 2: Sl st in each sc around, join with a sl st in first st of rnd; finish off.

Finishing: Refer to close-up photo ***(Fig. 19)*** for placement of facial features.

Sew eyes and mouth to head; with black yarn, embroider nose by working several satin sts.

Stuff head with polyester filling and sew to body.

Sew buttons to body approx 1" apart.

Fig. 19

HAT
Beg at top with black, ch 2.

Rnd 1: 8 Sc in 2nd ch from hook.

Rnd 2: 2 Sc in each sc around: 16 sc.

Rnd 3: Sc in each sc around.

Rnd 4: 2 Sc in each sc around: 32 sc.

Rnd 5: Sc in each sc around.

Rnd 6: ★ 2 sc in next sc, sc in next sc; rep from ★ around: 48 sc.

Rnd 7: Work a raised sc in each sc around.

Rnds 8-17: Sc in each sc around.

Rnd 18: ★ Sc in each of next 4 sc, 2 sc in next sc; rep from ★ 8 times **more**, ending with sc in each of last 3 sts: 57 sc.

Rnd 19: ★ Sc in each of next 3 sc, 2 sc in next sc; rep from ★ 13 times, sc in last sc: 71 sc.

Rnds 20-22: Sc in each sc around.

Rnd 23: Sl st in each st around, join with a sl st in first st of rnd; finish off.

Finishing: Roll last 3 rnds of hat to form brim. Stuff hat with polyester filling and sew to head.

ARMS (make 2)
With white, ch 2.

Rnd 1: 8 Sc in 2nd ch from hook.

Rnd 2: ★ 2 Sc in next sc, sc in next sc; rep from ★ around: 12 sc.

Rnds 3-27: Sc in each sc around.

Rnd 28: Sc in each of next 6 sc, sl st in each of next 2 sc; finish off.

Finishing: Stuff arms with polyester filling to within 1" of opening; tack to sides of body at shoulder and elbow (**approx middle of arm**).

SCARF
With green, ch 6.

Row 1: Dc in 4th ch from hook, dc in each of last 2 ch; ch 1, turn.

Rows 2-62: Dc in each dc across; ch 1, turn. At end of last row, do not ch 1; finish off.

Fringe: Cut 2½" strands of yarn; using 2 strands for each tassel of fringe, tie 4 tassels across each short end of scarf. Trim ends evenly and tie scarf around neck.

BROOM
Handle: Twist 6 pipecleaners tog.

Leaving a tail for weaving in later, with brown, make a slip knot and sl st onto pipecleaners. Sc closely around length of pipecleaners, working enough sts to cover pipecleaners completely, ending ch 1; break yarn, leaving a yarn tail for weaving.

Weave beg and end yarn tails, with yarn needle, into handle.

Brush: Cut 25, 3" strands of brown yarn, tie at center with a 6" length, to make a tassel for top of broom. Attach the 6" length to one end of broom handle.

Using a 36" strand of brown yarn, wind yarn around bottom of tassel until it forms a thick base; tie beg and end yarn tails tog and weave ends into base.

Sew top of broom handle to bottom of right hand and sew base of broom at right shoulder.

MRS. SNOWMAN

BODY

With white, ch 2 and rep **Rnds 1-10** of Mr. Snowman's Body.

Rnd 11: Sc in each sc around: 64 sc.

Rnd 12: Rep Rnd 12 of Mr. Snowman's Body.

Rnds 13-40: Sc in each sc around.

Rnd 41: ★ Sc in each of next 8 sc, dec; rep from ★ 5 times **more**, ending with sc in each of last 4 sc: 58 sc.

Rnd 42: Sc in each sc around.

INSERT COFFEE CAN with plastic lid at bottom.

Rnd 43: ★ Sc in each of next 7 sc, dec; rep from ★ 5 times **more**, ending sc in each of last 4 sc: 52 sc.

Rnds 44-46: Sc in each sc around.

Rnd 47: ★ Sc in each of next 6 sc, dec; rep from ★ 5 times **more**, ending sc in each of last 4 sc: 46 sc.

Rnd 48: Sc in each sc around.

Rnd 49: ★ Sc in each of next 5 sc, dec; rep from ★ 5 times **more**, ending sc in each of last 4 sc: 40 sc.

Rnd 50: Sc in each sc around.

Rnd 51: ★ Sc in each of next 8 sc, dec; rep from ★ 3 times **more**: 36 sc.

Rnd 52: Sc in each of next 36 sc, sl st in each of next 2 sc; finish off.

HEAD

With white, ch 2. Rep **Rnds 1-23** of Mr. Snowman's Head.

Mouth: With red, ch 10; finish off.

Buttons (make 2): With black, ch 2.

Rnd 1: 8 Sc in 2nd ch from hook.

Rnd 2: Sl st in each sc around, join with a sl st in first st of rnd; finish off.

Finishing: Refer to close-up photo ***(Fig. 20)*** for placement of facial features.

With double strand of black yarn, embroider a few satin sts for each eye and four straight sts for eyelashes.

With black, embroider nose by working several satin sts horizontally below center of eyes. Sew mouth to head.

Stuff head with polyester filling and sew to body.

Sew buttons to body approx 1½" apart.

HAT

Beg at top with black, ch 2.

Rnd 1: 8 Sc in 2nd ch from hook.

Rnd 2: 2 Sc in each sc around: 16 sc.

Rnd 3: ★ 2 Sc in next sc, sc in next sc; rep from ★ around: 24 sc.

Rnd 4: ★ 2 Sc in next sc, sc in each of next 2 sc; rep from ★ around: 32 sc.

Rnd 5: Sc in each sc around.

Rnd 6: ★ 2 Sc in next sc, sc in each of next 3 sc; rep from ★ around: 40 sc.

Rnd 7: Work a raised sc in each sc around.

Rnd 8: ★ 2 Sc in next sc, sc in each of next 4 sc; rep from ★ around: 48 sc.

Rnds 9-15: Sc in each sc around.

Rnd 16: ★ 2 Sc in next sc, sc in each of next 5 sc; rep from ★ around: 56 sc.

Rnds 17-20: Sc in each sc around.

Rnd 21: ★ Sc in next sc, work a double knot st (follow Pattern Stitch instructions in **Wreath Pattern** on page 4), sk 3 sc; rep from ★ around, ending by working a double knot st, join with a sl st in top knot of first double knot st of rnd.

Rnd 22: ★ Work a double knot st, sc in top knot of next double knot st of prev rnd; rep from ★ around, join with a sl st in first st of rnd; finish off.

Stuff hat with filling and sew onto head.

Fig. 20

ARMS (make 2)
With white, ch 2 and rep **Rnds 1-21** of Mr. Snowman's arms.

Rnd 22: Sc in each of next 6 sc, sl st in each of next 2 sc; finish off.

Stuff arms with filling to within 1" of opening; tack to sides of body at shoulder and elbow **(approx middle of arm)**.

SCARF
With red, ch 74 loosely. Sc in second ch from hook, work a double knot st, ★ sk 3 chs, sc in next ch, work a double knot st; rep from ★ 16 times **more**, sk 3 chs, sc in last ch. Now working into unworked loops at opposite side of beg ch-74, sc in same ch last sc was worked, work a double knot st, ★★ sk 3 chs, sc in next ch, work a double knot st; rep from ★★ 17 times **more**, join with a sl st in beg sc: 36 double knot sts.

Tie scarf around neck.

WREATH
Make a 1½" diameter circle with one 6" pipecleaner. With green yarn, make a slip knot and sl st onto circle; draw up a 1" loop. ★ Hold loop with your left hand; remove crochet hook from work; with your right hand, wrap the yarn from the left to the right around the bottom of the loop just pulled up, (yarn will now be in the back of the circle). Insert hook back into loop just made; insert hook into circle and draw up another 1" loop; rep from ★ until entire circle is filled with loop stitches. After completing the last loop st, draw up a loop with your crochet hook and make a sl st. Finish off.

Finishing: With a 6" strand of red yarn, make a bow and sew it to wreath at bottom. Sew sides of wreath to ends of arms.

10 SANTA PILLOW

designed by Barbara Luoma; Mundelein, IL

Materials: Worsted wt yarn, 4 oz green, 2 oz red, 1 oz **each** white and pink, 1 yd black; aluminum crochet hook sizes E and F (Canadian sizes 9 and 8) or sizes needed for gauge; polyester filling for stuffing; 12" diameter pillow form; sewing thread for finishing.

Gauge: With smaller hook,
in sc, 10 sts = 2"; 11 rows = 2"
With larger hook,
in dc, 5 sts= 1"; 2 rows = 1"

PILLOW COVER

BACK
With green and larger hook, ch 2.

Rnd 1: Work 7 sc in 2nd ch from hook, join with a sl st in first sc.

Rnd 2: Ch 3 (counts as one dc), dc in base of ch, 2 dc in next sc and in each sc around: 14 dc.

NOTE: At the end of this rnd and all following rnds, join with a sl st in top of beg ch. Joining method will not be mentioned again.

Rnd 3: Ch 3, dc in base of ch, 2 dc in next dc and in each dc around: 28 dc.

Rnd 4: Ch 3, dc in base of ch, 2 dc in next dc and in each dc around: 56 dc.

Rnds 5 and 6: Ch 3, dc in next dc and in each dc around: 56 dc.

Rnd 7: Ch 3, dc in base of ch, dc in next dc, ★ 2 dc in next dc, dc in next dc; rep from ★ around: 84 dc.

Rnd 8: Ch 3, dc in each dc around.

Rnd 9: Ch 3, dc in base of ch, dc in next dc, ★ 2 dc in next dc, dc in next dc; rep from ★ around: 126 dc.

Rnds 10-14: Ch 3, dc in next dc and in each dc around.

Finish off.

FRONT
Rep instructions for Back.

SANTA CLAUS APPLIQUE

Santa Face: With pink and smaller hook, ch 12.

Row 1: Sc in 2nd ch from hook and in each ch across; ch 1, turn: 11 sc.

Rows 2-10: 2 Sc in first sc, sc in each sc across to last sc, 2 sc in last sc; ch 1, turn. At end of Row 10, you should have 29 sc.

Rows 11-19: Sc in each sc across; ch 1, turn. At end of last row, do not ch 1. Finish off pink; join red with a sl st in same sp.

Hat: Row 1: Ch 3 (counts as a dc), turn. Dc in next st and in each st across: 29 dc.

Rows 2-3: Ch 3, turn. Dc in next dc and in each dc across, ending dc in top of turning ch: 29 dc.

Row 4: Ch 2, turn. Dec over next 2 dc, dc in next dc and in each dc across to within last 2 dc, dec over last 2 dc, dc in top of turning ch: 27 dc **(counting turning ch as one dc)**.

Rows 5-8: Ch 2, turn. Dec over next 2 dc, dc in next dc and in each dc across to within last 2 dc, dec over last 2 dc, dc in top of turning ch. At end of Row 8, you should have 19 dc.

Row 9: Ch 2, turn. Dec over next 2 dc, dc in next dc and in each dc to within last 2 dc, dec, dc in top of turning ch; ch 12, join with a sl st in top of ch-2 at beg of row to form a ring.

Rnd 10: Sc in same sp as joining, sc in each dc and in each ch st around: 29 sc.

NOTE: At end of this rnd and following rnds, ***do not*** *join; mark beg of each rnd and move marker at end of each rnd. Marking will not be mentioned again.*

Rnds 11-16: Sc in each sc around.

Rnd 17: Sc in each sc around, dec 5 sts evenly spaced: 24 sc.

Rnds 18-29: Sc in each sc around.

Rnd 30: Sc in each sc around, dec 5 sts evenly spaced: 19 sc.

Rnds 31-34: Sc in each sc around.

Rnd 35: Sc in each sc around, dec 5 sts evenly spaced: 14 sc.

Rnds 36-39: Sc in each sc around.

Rnd 40: (Dec over next 2 sts) 7 times: 7 sc.

Finish off, leaving 12" length; thread yarn needle, weave through sts and draw up tightly to close.

Hat Band: With white and larger hook, ch 27.

Row 1: Sc in 2nd ch from hook and in each rem ch across: 26 sc.

Rows 2 and 3: Ch 3 (counts as one dc), dc in next st and in each st across: 26 dc.

Row 4: Ch 1, sc in next dc and in each dc across. Finish off.

Eyes (make 2): With white and smaller hook, ch 2. Work 5 hdc in 2nd ch from hook; finish off.

Moustache: With white and smaller hook, ch 13. Sl st in 2nd ch from hook, sl st in each of next 2 chs, hdc in each of next 6 ch, sl st in each of rem 3 chs. Finish off.

Pompons (make 9): Following instructions on page 3, make 9 fat 1½" diameter pompons.

Finishing: Refer to close-up photo ***(Fig. 21)*** as a guide for placement of facial features.

Sew eyes on face, working one french knot with black at center of each eye.

With pink yarn, work several straight sts horizontally for nose. Sew moustache below nose, turning up slightly at corners; at midpoint, sew and draw tog center sts just below nose.

With red yarn, work a few straight sts for mouth. Sew hat band to hat. Sew one pompon to tip of hat. Stuff face and part of hat, sew to pillow cover, turning edges under. String rem 8 pompons tog and sew to bottom of face for beard.

Sl st front and back pieces tog over pillow form, working with larger hook and green yarn and carefully matching sts. Finish off.

Fig. 21

11 CHRISTMAS STOCKING

designed by Barbara Johnston; Los Gatos, CA

Materials: Worsted wt yarn, 6 oz green, 2 oz white; sport wt yarn, few yds red for embroidery; aluminum crochet hook size E (Canadian size 9) or size needed for gauge.

Gauge: In sc, 4 sts = 1"; 4½ rows = 1"

INSTRUCTIONS

BACK

With green, ch 9.

Row 1: Sc in 2nd ch from hook and in each ch across; ch 1, turn: 8 sc.

Row 2: 2 Sc in first sc, sc in each sc across; ch 6, turn: 9 sc.

Row 3: Sc in 2nd ch from hook, sc in each rem ch, sc in each sc to within last st, 2 sc in last sc; ch 1, turn: 15 sc.

Row 4: 2 Sc in first sc, sc in each sc across; ch 6, turn: 16 sc.

Row 5: Sc in 2nd ch from hook, sc in each rem ch, sc in each sc to within last st, 2 sc in last sc; ch 1, turn: 22 sc.

Row 6: 2 Sc in first sc, sc in each sc across; ch 4, turn: 23 sc.

Row 7: Sc in 2nd ch from hook, sc in each rem ch, sc in each sc to within last st, 2 sc in last sc; ch 1, turn: 27 sc.

Row 8: 2 sc in first sc, sc in each sc across; ch 3, turn: 28 sc.

Row 9: Sc in 2nd ch from hook, sc in each rem ch, sc in each sc to within last st, 2 sc in last sc; ch 1, turn: 31 sc.

Row 10: Sc in each sc across; ch 1, turn.

Row 11: 2 Sc in first sc, sc in each sc across; ch 1, turn: 32 sc.

Row 12: Sc in each sc across; ch 1, turn.

Rows 13-16: Rep Rows 11 and 12 twice: At end of Rnd 16, you should have 34 sc.

Row 17: 2 Sc in first sc, sc in each sc to within 3 sc of end, dec over next 2 sc, sc in last sc; ch 1, turn: 34 sc.

Row 18: Sc in each sc across; ch 1, turn.

Row 19: 2 Sc in first sc, sc in each sc to within 2 sc of end, sk last 2 sc; ch 1, turn: 33 sc.

Row 20: Sc in each sc across; ch 1, turn.

Row 21: Sc in each sc to within 2 sc of end, sk last 2 sc; ch 1, turn: 31 sc.

Rows 22 and 23: Rep Rows 20 and 21: 29 sc.

Row 24: Sc in each sc to within 3 sc of end, dec over next 2 sc, sc in last sc; ch 1, turn: 28 sc.

Row 25: Sc in each sc to within 2 sc of end, sk last 2 sc; ch 1, turn: 26 sc.

Rows 26-29: Rep Rows 24 and 25 twice. At end of Row 29, you should have 20 sc.

Rows 30-38: Sc in each sc across; ch 1, turn.

Row 39: 2 Sc in first sc, sc in each sc across; ch 1, turn: 21 sc.

Row 40: Sc in each sc across; ch 1, turn.

Rows 41-43: Rep Rows 39 and 40 once, then rep Row 39 once **more**. At end of Row 43, you should have 23 sc.

Rows 44-46: Sc in each sc across; ch 1, turn.

Row 47: 2 Sc in first sc, sc in each sc across; ch 1, turn: 24 sc.

Rows 48-51: Rep Rows 44-47: At end of Row 51, you should have 25 sc.

Rows 52-56: Sc in each sc across; ch 1, turn.

Row 57: 2 Sc in first sc, sc in each sc across; ch 1, turn: 26 sc.

Rows 58-75: Rep Rows 57-62, 3 times: At end of Row 75, you should have 29 sc.

Row 76: Sc in each sc across; ch 1, turn.

Row 77: Sc in each sc across to within last st; in last st work sc until 2 loops rem on hook, change to white and complete st; ch 1, turn. Finish off green.

Row 78: With white, sc in first sc, ★ sc in next st **in row below**, sc in next st **in second row below**, sc in next st **in row below**, sc in each of next 3 sc; rep from ★ across, ending last rep sc in last sc; ch 1, turn: 29 sts.

Row 79: Sc in each sc across; ch 3, turn.

Row 80: Work (hdc in next sc, sc in next sc, hdc in next sc, dc in each of next 2 sc) 5 times, hdc in next sc, sc in next sc, hdc in next sc, dc in last sc; ch 1, turn.

Row 81: Sl st in each st across, ending sl st in top of turning ch. Finish off.

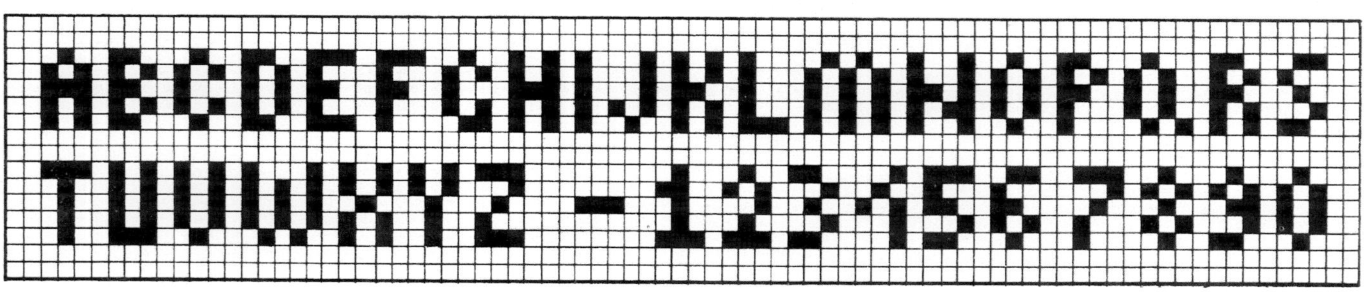

FRONT
With green, ch 9.

Rows 1-7: Rep Rows 1-7 of Back.

Row 8: 2 Sc in first sc, sc in each sc across to last st; in last st work sc until 2 loops rem on hook, change to white and complete st. Finish off green; ch 3, turn.

Rows 9-19: With white, rep Rows 9-19 of Back.

Row 20: Sc in each sc across to last st; work sc in last st, changing to green when 2 loops rem on hook; ch 1, turn. Finish off white.

Rows 21-76: Rep Rows 21-76 of Back.

Row 77: Sc in each sc across. Finish off green.

Row 78: Join white with a sl st in beg sc of prev row, sc in same st, ★ sc in next st **in row below**, sc in next st **in 2nd row below**, sc in next st **in row below**, sc in each of next 3 sc; rep from ★ across, ending last rep sc in last sc; ch 1, turn: 29 sc.

Rows 79-81: Rep Rows 79-81 of Back. Finish off.

Embroidery: With red sport wt yarn, work name or initials in cross stitch, using alphabet chart, page 18; take care to center letters on white band of Front. One square on chart equals one sc on stocking.

FINISHING
Back: Leaving scalloped edge at top unworked, work one row of sc around entire edge of stocking. Beg at upper left-hand corner, work 4 sc in white; change to green and work into sc rows around to upper right-hand corner; change to white, work 4 sc in white. Finish off.

Front: Work Front to correspond with Back, making sure to have the same number of sts as on the back, changing to white for white band rows. Hold wrong sides of front and back tog with right side of front facing you, sl st around through both pieces, matching sts carefully. Finish off.

Hanger: With white, ch 18, sl st loosely in second ch from hook and in each rem ch. Finish off; fold in half and sew ends to stocking.

CHRISTMAS STOCKING APPLIQUÉS

Materials: Sport wt yarn, 1 oz red, several yds each pink and white, 1 yd black; aluminum crochet hook size E (Canadian size 9); sewing thread for finishing.

Gauge: In sc, 6 sts = 1"; 6 rows = 1"

STAR

With red, ★ ch 5, sl st in 2nd ch from hook, hdc in next ch, dc in each of last 2 ch; rep from ★ 4 times **more**, join with a sl st in first ch of beg ch. Finish off. Sew applique to stocking.

PINE TREE

Row 1 (right side): With white, ch 13. Dc in one loop only of 4th ch from hook (counts as first dc), dc in one loop only of each rem ch across; ch 1, turn: 11 dc.

Row 2: Work a raised sc in next dc and in each dc across (working into bars of dc and following instructions for raised sc in the **Mr. & Mrs. Snowman Patt** on page 13); ch 2, turn: 10 sc.

Row 3: Dc in each of next 3 sts, dec, dc in each of next 4 sts; ch 1, turn: 9 sts, counting turning ch as one st.

Row 4: Work a raised sc in next st and in each st across; ch 1, turn: 8 sc.

Row 5: Sc in first sc and in each sc across; ch 1, turn: 8 sc.

Row 6: Work a raised sc in next st and in each st across ending sc in turning ch; ch 1, turn: 8 sc.

Row 7: Sk first sc, sc in each of next 2 sts, dec, sc in each of next 3 sts; ch 1, turn: 6 sc.

Row 8: Rep Row 6: 6 sc.

Row 9: Sk first sc, sc in next sc, dec, sc in each of next 2 sc; ch 1, turn: 5 sc.

Row 10: Rep Row 6: 4 sc.

Row 11: Sk first sc, dec over next 2 sts, sc in next st; turn: 3 sc.

Row 12: Dec over next 2 sts, sc in next st; turn: 2 sc.

Row 13: Insert hook in dec st and draw up a loop, insert hook in next st and draw up a loop; YO and draw through all 3 loops on hook. Finish off.

Tree Trunk: Beg at bottom of tree, with right side facing, join white with a sl st in 5th ch of beg ch-13 (base ch).

Row 1: Ch 3, sc in 2nd ch from hook, sc in next ch, join with a sl st in 6th ch of base ch; turn.

Row 2: Sc in each of next 2 sc; ch 1, turn.

Row 3: Sc in each of next 2 sc, join with a sl st in 7th ch of base ch. Finish off.

Sew applique to stocking.

SANTA CLAUS
BODY
With red, wind yarn around finger once to form a loop.

Rnd 1: Sl st into loop, work 6 sc in loop, join with a sl st in beg sc. Now draw loop closed by pulling beg yarn tail.

Rnd 2: Sc in same st as joining, 2 sc in next sc, ★ sc in next sc, 2 sc in next sc; rep from ★ around, join with a sl st in beg sc of rnd: 12 sc.

Rnd 3: Sc in same st as joining, sc in next sc, 2 sc in next sc, ★ sc in each of next 2 sc, 2 sc in next sc; rep from ★ around, join with a sl st in beg sc of rnd: 16 sc.

Rnds 4-6: Rep Rnds 2 and 3 once, then rep Rnd 2 once more: At end of Rnd 6 you should have 48 sc.

Rnd 7: Sc in next sc and in each sc around, do **not** join.

Rnd 8: Sl st in back loop of each of next 45 sc; change to pink, finish off red, ch 1, sc in each of next 3 sts; ch 1, turn.

HEAD

Row 1 (wrong side): Continuing with pink, 2 sc in first sc, sc in next sc, 2 sc in next sc; ch 1, turn: 5 sc.

Rows 2-4: 2 Sc in first sc, sc in each sc to last sc, 2 sc in last sc; ch 1, turn: 11 sc at end of Row 4.

Rows 5 and 6: Sc in each sc across; ch 1, turn.

Row 7: Dec over first 2 sc, sc in each sc to within 2 sc of end, dec over last 2 sc: 9 sc. Finish off.

HAT BAND & BEARD

With right side facing, join white with a sl st in first dec st at upper, right-hand corner of face. Ch 2, hdc in same st, hdc in each st across to last st, ch 2, sl st in same st. Turning work slightly clockwise, sc in side of each end st of next 5 rows of face, 2 hdc in side of end st of next row. Now fold your work so that wrong sides of body and face are tog. With right side of face facing you, and working through both pieces, 2 dc in next sc, 2 tr in next sc, 2 dc in next sc. Continuing in sides of rows on face only, 2 hdc in side of next row, sc in side of each of next 5 rows; join with a sl st in beg sl st at upper, right-hand corner. Finish off.

HAT

With wrong side facing and hat band across top, join red with a sl st in first hdc at upper, right-hand corner.

Row 1: Sc in same st as joining, sc in each of next 2 sts, hdc in each of next 2 sts, dc in each of next 2 sts, 2 tr in next st; ch 1, turn: 9 sts.

Rows 2, 4 and 6: Sc in each of next 8 sts, sl st in next st; ch 1, turn.

Rows 3, 5 and 7: Sk first st, sc in each of next 2 sts, hdc in each of next 2 sts, dc in each of next 2 sts, 2 tr in each of next 2 sts; ch 1, turn.

Row 8: Sl st in each st across and in end sts of each row of hat to hat band. Join with a sl st at hat band; finish off.

Finishing: Make a 1" diameter pompon, following instructions on page 3, and attach to tip of hat. Refer to photo as a guide for embroidery. With single strand of black, work one cross st for each eye and one french knot for each button on body. With 2 strands of red, work one french knot for nose. Sew applique to stocking.

12 CHRISTMAS GLASS JACKET

designed by Janice Tessitore; Palatine, IL

Size: Fits 2½" diameter glass

Materials: Sport wt yarn, 1 oz red; aluminum crochet hook size F (Canadian size 8) or size needed for gauge.

Gauge: In sc, 5 sts = 1"; 7 rnds = 1"

INSTRUCTIONS

Wind yarn around finger once to form a loop.

Rnd 1: Sl st into loop, work 6 sc in loop, join with a sl st in beg sc. Now draw up loop by pulling tail end of yarn.

Rnd 2: 2 Sc in each sc around: 12 sc.

NOTE: On this rnd and following rnds, ***do not*** *join rnds unless otherwise specified; mark beg of each rnd and move marker at end of each rnd.*

Rnd 3: ★ 2 Sc in next sc, sc in next sc; rep from ★ around: 18 sc.

Rnd 4: ★ 2 sc in next sc, sc in each of next 2 sc; rep from ★ around: 24 sc.

Rnd 5: ★ 2 Sc in next sc, sc in each of next 3 sc; rep from ★ around: 30 sc.

Rnd 6: ★ 2 sc in next sc, sc in each of next 4 sc; rep from ★ around: 36 sc.

Rnd 7: ★ 2 Sc in next sc, sc in each of next 5 sc; rep from ★ around: 42 sc.

Rnd 8: Sc in each sc around, join with a sl st in beg sc of rnd; ch 1, turn.

Rnd 9: Work a raised sc loosely in each sc around. (Refer to instructions for raised sc in **Mr. & Mrs. Snowman Patt** on page 13.) Join with a sl st in beg st of rnd; turn.

Rnds 10-29: Sc in each sc around: 42 sc.

Rnd 30: Sl st in each st around, join with a sl st in beg st of rnd. Finish off.

HOLLY WREATH APPLIQUE

Materials: Sport wt yarn, few yds of green; aluminum crochet hook size D (Canadian size 10); 8" length of ¼" red ribbon; 21 red beads; small safety pin; sewing thread for finishing.

Gauge: None specified

INSTRUCTIONS

Ch 12, join with a sl st to form a ring.

Rnd 1: Work 30 sc in ring, join with a sl st in beg sc of rnd.

Rnds 2 and 3: Sc in first sc and in each sc around, join with a sl st in beg sc of rnd.

Rnd 4: Sl st in each st around, join with a sl st in beg st of rnd. Finish off.

Finishing: To form berries, sew groups of 3 red beads, evenly spaced, around wreath. Tie ribbon in a bow and sew to wreath. Trim ends evenly. Sew back of safety pin to back of wreath. Pin wreath to glass jacket.